PRAYING OUR GRIEF

Comfort and Prayers for Widows

•

Linda Perrone Rooney

Resurrection Press
An Imprint of
CATHOLIC BOOK PUBLISHING CORP.
Totowa • New Jersey

First published in April, 2008 by
Catholic Book Publishing/Resurrection Press
77 West End Road
Totowa, NJ 07512

ISBN 978-1-933066-09-7

Library of Congress Catalog Number 2007940983

Cover design by Geoffrey Butz

Printed in the United States of America.

3 4 5 6 7 8 9

www.catholicbookpublishing.com

Contents

Introduction

Every widow's experience of her husband's death is unique and unrepeatable. Mine is no different. Yet it is my hope that the reflections, prayers and actions offered in this small volume will speak to other widows. My own journey is ongoing and each day I learn something new about myself, about mourning and about the God who brings life out of death. It is my hope that regardless of how long you have been a widow, and especially if it is recent, you will find support, wisdom and comfort in this book

Praying Our Grief: Comfort and Prayers for Widows, is designed to be read in whatever order most suits your need. A quick glance at the table of contents may point you to a current experience or concern. Start there. Or, read the book from beginning to end and prepare yourself for experiences you have not yet had. That's a good approach as well. Don't try to "go it alone." In the privacy of your own home, let this book be a friend, a spiritual guide and a healing aid.

Once you have chosen a chapter to use, take time to actually do the action. Sit with the scripture and let it speak to you. Write your thoughts in a journal without censuring them. Use the prayer to help you express your own heart's intention or as a model for developing your prayers. Any and all that is contained in each chapter can assist you through this time of upheaval.

Know full well and take comfort in the fact that you have joined a company of women whose greatest desire is for your wholeness and peace.

Linda Rooney

I Can't Believe This Is Happening

"*W*hy did this happen now?" The reality for those who grieve is that there is no good time for someone you love to die, leaving you to face a world in which they have ceased to be present. Even when the mind comprehends that everyone dies, the heart and spirit shrink from such a personal blow.

Widows, while no exception to this experience of shock, grieve in a unique way because of the intimacy and vulnerability that marriage entails; two lives are entangled and dependent, at all levels.

Letting go of a life-partner with whom you have shared an enriching and powerful exchange of love is heart-breaking. For those whose marriage was difficult or disappointing, the heartbreak remains, because anyone who has struggled to build a successful marriage clings to the hope that it will one day happen. Death deals a fatal blow to those dreams.

Whether he died after a prolonged illness, or suddenly, without warning, it's normal to experience a sense of disbelief in the face of a husband's death. This denial doesn't necessarily leave in the first hours or days, so be gentle with yourself as your new reality is revealed to you.

Action

Accept any feelings of disbelief and let them be. Don't think critical thoughts of yourself. Do what you need to do, each day, and the reality of your loss will settle in, taking you a step forward on your grief journey.

Prayer

Dear Lord, how can this be? It can't be true that my husband is dead. I think I hear his voice. I wake up eager to talk to him. Did he think of me before he died? Why didn't we have more time to say the things that needed saying, to do what we always talked about but never did? Why, Lord, why now? Give me the courage to accept his death and to face that I will never see my husband again on this earth. Help me to let him go. Amen.

Scripture for Reflection

For I, the Lord, your God, hold your right hand; it is I who say to you, "Do not fear, I will help you."

Isaiah 41:13

Journaling

What thoughts, feelings and prayers are in your heart right now?

Making Funeral Arrangements

*I*n years gone by burying the dead was a more intimate affair. Through the loving, hands-on ministry of family, the body was washed and dressed, the parlor prepared for visitors, food and drink were brought by neighbors and their chatter, stories, tears and laughter embraced both the dead and those who mourned. Finally, after prayers and rituals, everyone, carrying the body, walked to the cemetery for the final goodbye.

Today, making funeral arrangements is a complicated, expensive, "antiseptic" experience. It often lacks personal intimacy and loving interaction with the one who has died. Funerals are big business, at their worst, rather than a support for family rituals performed as final acts of love.

You are asked to make funeral arrangements when you are least focused, and most befuddled. You are submerged in details and choices when what you need is a place of quiet where you can gather your thoughts and absorb the blow you have been dealt. You'll get through it, but hold on to the truth that this funeral is your last act of love. Make it personal . . . something you'll be proud to remember and which will help you to engage your grief in a healing way.

Action

Before anyone or anything distracts you, take time to determine what you believe will best celebrate your husband's return to the Lord. Do you want to help dress the body? Should family members have roles during the services? Will pictures and mementos be displayed during visitation? Will the casket be closed or open? Think and pray about what is most meaningful to you and then expect to have those wishes fulfilled.

Prayer

Dear Lord, making these arrangements is not something I ever expected to do. I want to give my beloved a meaningful and loving final tribute—not be overwhelmed by choices and opinions. Guide my thoughts and free my heart to surface its deepest desires. Clear my mind for wise decisions and give me the words that will send my husband forward in grace and peace surrounded by our loving thoughts and gestures. Amen.

Scripture for Reflection

O Lord, give heed to my prayer; let my plea for help reach you. Do not conceal your face from my sight in the time of my distress. Incline your ear to me; on the day when I call out to you answer me speedily.   Psalms 102:1-2

Journaling

What thoughts, feelings and prayers are in your heart right now?

Facing Family and Friends

*N*o one wants to go through the experience of a husband's death alone. The lucky ones have family and friends who reach out with support. Yet, even their sympathy and sincere expression of feelings can make you feel overwhelmed and pressed to "be strong."

Families and friends mean well and try to do what they think will help. What they can't realize is the depth of the wound that a husband's death inflicts. Tidying up the finances, cleaning out the closets, looking at old snapshots and listening to stories for the "nth" time is helpful, but it does not heal. Invitations that will "get her out of the house" and "take her mind off of it," in truth, only emphasize that what was two is now one. What can you do?

As a widow you will learn that the only choice that ultimately brings peace is walking the path of grief that has your name on it. The only way to walk with grief is to meet it head on and know that those who have walked before you have survived.

Action

Be gracious when invitations come, but only go if you truly want to go. Be grateful when family or friends call, help with difficult tasks or spend time listening, but feel free to turn down their offers, to claim your solitude, and to move at the pace that feels right *for you*. This is your grief and you are the only one who can determine how to handle it.

Prayer

Gracious God, I need your kindness today. I need the backbone to say "no" to invitations I don't want to accept— but in a way that shows I am pleased to be asked. I need the right words to tell my family why their ideas, advice and "answers to my problems" are gratefully received but not what I am about to do. Give me wisdom to know when to participate and when to seek solitude. Give me the courage of my convictions and the ability to listen to the needs of my own heart. Amen.

Scripture for Reflection

The Israelites wept for Moses in the plains of Moab thirty days; then the period of mourning for Moses was ended.
Deuteronomy 34:8

Journaling

What thoughts, feelings and prayers are in your heart right now?

Speaking the "D" Word

*E*uphemisms abound when people talk about death. They say "passed on, sleeps in the Lord, is in a better place, slipped away" and any number of other things instead of, "died." What's wrong with the honest, non-sugar-coated reality of death? Even some widows speak of their dead husbands without ever using the word that most describes him now—dead. Is loneliness easier to bear if you say, "he has passed on," instead of died? Will it dry the fountain of tears ready to overflow at any moment to say, "he is in a better place," rather than, he is dead?

People of faith know that because of Jesus Christ, death is not the final answer. With faith, you accept that your husband has gone before you to prepare a place of peace. In faith, believers understand that death is as much a part of the human and spiritual journey as is birth, and in the end, it will lead to a rebirth the likes of which we cannot imagine.

Don't get caught up in the world's attempts to deny death. Use the "d" word to support your own grasp on reality and as a sign of your faith in the life to come.

Action

Whenever you find yourself avoiding the words die, death and dead, stop—smile, and then use the "d" word, instead. Remember that Jesus "died" on the cross, he didn't "pass away." His "death" brought life—a life you share in now and in the world to come.

Prayer

Jesus, I know you died on the cross because you love me. Your death brought me salvation; and your rising from the dead gives me the chance to have new life. After the small deaths of daily life and in the end, when my own death comes, bring me into your loving embrace forever. In the meantime, take away my fear of death, my reluctance to speak of it, my struggle to look it in the face and believe that you have given me victory over it. Amen.

Scripture for Reflection

Death has been swallowed up in victory. Where, O death, is your victory? Where, O death, is your sting?

1 Corinthians 15:54-55

Journaling

What thoughts, feelings and prayers are in your heart right now?

Remembering the Past

*W*idows have plenty of time to remember. Throughout your mourning, memories will yearn to be reviewed, analyzed, treasured or discarded. Mental pictures and inner feelings pop up when least expected and they aren't put aside easily. They clamor for attention, and some days lingering over your memories seems to be all that you can do. The mind is a file box cataloging all the moments spent living with and loving another person. While this can be a sentimental journey, it can also be a difficult reliving of the past. You need to decide whether your memories are a supportive mental and emotional scrapbook of your married life; or, a hurtful, painful collage of regrets that leave you debilitated and bitter.

Every marriage has memories of difficult times, hurtful words or choices that brought negative consequences. On the other hand, each marriage produces moments of happiness, tenderness, mutual giving and love. Which memories you choose to keep on file will determine how you prepare yourself to embrace your future.

Action

As you reflect on a memory, decide whether it is one worthy of keeping. If positive, write it down or place it, with a picture, in a scrapbook. If it is dispiriting, let it go. Keep only those memories that give you life.

Prayer

Dear Lord Jesus, I want to remember my husband and our years together in the light of your mercy and love. Take away all guilt, bitterness or anger that clings to my memories. I release him into your arms without regret. Fill my mind with memories of joy—the beautiful moments, the tender embraces, happy, silly, precious snapshots of a full life, lived by two human beings, who tried their best. Amen.

Scripture for Reflection

Watch yourselves closely, so as neither to forget the things that your eyes have seen nor to let them slip from your mind all the days of your life.　　　　Deuteronomy 4:9

Journaling

What thoughts, feelings and prayers are in your heart right now?

The Need for Solitude

*E*very person experiences being alone and loneliness.

Aloneness is being in a space without another person present. It has no emotional overtones. Sometimes we simply want to be alone. Loneliness is marked by a sense of imposed, not chosen, isolation. It is a negative experience of aloneness.

Solitude, being alone without being lonely, is a positive, constructive state of interaction with yourself. Solitude provides time for reflection, inner searching, growth and enjoyment. It is a way to take pleasure in your own space and whatever it holds; an opportunity to renew yourself. Widows often have alone time that they experience as loneliness because they haven't found the key to solitude. They may see aloneness as a curse—something they don't want; instead of an opportunity—time to enter within and meet a new friend.

Solitude becomes a blessing when we become friends with ourselves and allow that friendship to provide the company we need. Self-awareness and inner peace are found in solitude.

Action

The next time you are alone and lonely, remind yourself that this is an opportunity to grow, to consciously seek solitude. Take whatever thoughts or feelings are dragging you down and turn them "right side up" to find their positive value. If you feel sad, seek to understand the source of that sadness while naming things that bring you joy. If you feel isolated, think of people who have reached out to you today and what a gift that was. Create solitude.

Prayer

Ever present God, fill me with the knowledge of your presence. Shower me with a heart for reflection and an inner vision to recognize all the blessed love that surrounds me. Help me to love myself and to consider my own company enough. Let me see that loneliness is my enemy but solitude, which I can create, is my friend and a gift you have given me so that I may grow to know and love myself and you more. Amen.

Scripture for Reflection

The Lord remains close to the brokenhearted, and he saves those whose spirit is crushed.   Psalms 34:19

Journaling

What thoughts, feelings and prayers are in your heart right now?

A Quiet House

A house's silence can be so loud it thunders. Even with people around, the place that your husband filled creates a vacuum, cutting you off from yourself unless you know how to tame it.

Taming silence doesn't mean displacing it with noise. Taming silence is not running the TV or radio from morning 'til night just to hear a sound of life. No, taming silence happens when you befriend it—when you embrace it as a blessing, making it a welcome companion.

A quiet house gives you room to heal. It doesn't distract from your pain, or block the insights trying to surface in your heart. A quiet house wraps its arms around you, creating a safe place for your tears; a familiar place to spill your thoughts and fears; an open space to hold all the treasures of your memories.

Don't fear a quiet house. Instead, give thanks and rejoice that you have a place ready to receive your grief and to assist you in your healing.

Action

When tempted to fill your house with noise in order to distract you from your pain and grief, remember the blessings of the quiet house—walk around each room and touch the walls, the furniture, the very air, acknowledging that the Spirit of God is present here and too, the spirit of the one you love—both come to comfort you in the stillness.

Prayer

Spirit of Stillness, hover over me. Enfold me in your wings of peace and comfort. Make my heart glad for the silence and pour on me the threefold blessing of the quiet house: tears, inner conversation, and treasured memories. Amen.

Scripture for Reflection

Be still and acknowledge that I am God.   Psalms 46:11

Journaling

What thoughts, feelings and prayers are in your heart right now?

God's Time

*I*f only you could embrace time in the way of the ancient Greeks. They used two words for time: *chronos* and *kairos*. *Chronos* means "clock" time—the way you measure hours, days and years. It's *chronos* time we mark with our watches and calendars and lament when we've missed a special date or come late to an event. *Kairos* refers to God's time—eternal time. It cannot be measured or anticipated.

When your husband dies, chronological time collides with God's time. To look at the calendar then, is to feel cheated and perhaps, angry, especially if he died at a time of heightened family awareness like a holiday, an anniversary, the day he retired or a child's birthday or marriage. Why didn't God wait a little longer, we ask. Why should this date forever be associated with death?

But death resides in *kairos* time. When your husband died, he did not "run out of time." Rather, he entered into God's time, where there are no clocks, no calendars, no deadlines. Here, every moment is a special occasion. He is no longer "pressed for time" because time no longer exists. God's time is eternally the present and every moment of our living and dying is wrapped within it.

Action

Instead of saying that your husband died, at "this time, on this day" begin to say that he entered into God's time of immeasurable happiness and peace. Notice how this changes your own perspective on time.

Prayer

Eternal God, you who live in unmeasured time, fold your arms around my husband as he enters your forever-presence. Wrap me, too, in your embrace. Encase me in peace so that I am no longer fretful about the hours of the day or the future that knocks at my door. I long to set aside my watch and its calculated pace and to enjoy, instead, your open-ended contentment with each passing breath of life. Amen.

Scripture for Reflection

As for the exact day and hour, no one knows, neither the angels in heaven, nor the Son, but only the Father.

Matthew 24:36

Journaling

What thoughts, feelings and prayers are in your heart right now?

Sleeplessness

*C*hanges in eating and sleeping patterns are normal for those who grieve and especially for widows who are accustomed to preparing meals for and sleeping with another person. Sleeplessness, in particular, is difficult to combat, because the more exhausted you become from irregular or interrupted sleep or worse, chronic insomnia, the more your mental and spiritual health suffers. Sleeplessness nurtures a vicious cycle of depression and ill-health which in turn perpetuates the inability to sleep. Breaking this cycle isn't easy, but it is possible if you're willing to do the right things.

Some ways to break the cycle include: eating a balanced diet, exercising daily, seeing a counselor to discuss emotional problems, getting affairs squared away, going to bed at the same time each night, and establishing a daily spiritual routine.

You may notice a change in sleep patterns just after the death, about six months later and surrounding any major anniversaries during the first year. Chronic insomnia or the inability to break the cycle and function normally calls for a visit to the doctor for a thorough physical.

Sleeplessness doesn't have to contribute to ill-health or spiritual ennui. Do what you need to do to give your broken spirit a chance to recover. Do this exercise as often as necessary:

Close your eyes, inhale deeply through your nose and hold it for a count of 8, then exhale slowly through your mouth. Continue to do this slowly until you find rest.

Action

Once your husband is buried and the immediate tasks are addressed, make a doctor's appointment for a complete physical. Grief work is hard work and often during this time, widows experience health problems. Prevention is the best medicine.

Prayer

Dear Jesus, I remember your prayer in the Garden of Olives. Sleepless while all your disciples slept around you, you cried out to your Father for mercy. I cry to you, now. Create in me a heart at peace. Help me to trust that you will take care of me. Slow my breathing, relax my body, rock me in your arms until the sleep that hides from me—overcomes me, and I can rest, peacefully, ready to embrace another day. Amen.

Scripture for Reflection

I am exhausted from my sighing; every night I flood my bed with my tears, and I soak my couch with my weeping. My eyes grow dim because of my grief . . . the Lord has heard the sound of my weeping . . . the Lord has accepted my prayer.

Psalms 6:7-10

Journaling

What thoughts, feelings and prayers are in your heart right now?

—10—

Conquering Anxiety

nxiety is free-flowing fear, able to adhere to anything that crosses its path. Everyday life does have cause for anxiety, so not all anxiety is problematic. Sometimes, it's a powerful internal alarm that warns you that something "just isn't right." Learn to know the difference between this helpful anxiety and that which can riddle your life with unnecessary fear.

Widows are often anxious about home security, even when there's an alarm system. Or, you might worry about finances, being alone, coping with daily life, finding things to do with your time, your children—young or grown, if the car will break down. The list is endless.

Unproductive anxiety stems from lack of self-confidence and personal security. When a spouse dies, the carpet is pulled out from beneath the life that you were living and envisioned. Suddenly, all responsibilities are on your shoulders—not shared with another. It can seem overwhelming, and without an objective look at each issue as it arises, meeting the challenges can produce anxiety that can paralyze you.

Feelings of anxiety are real, but they aren't always factual. In order to move forward, you need to face your fears and deal with those that are real—dismissing the others.

Action

When the butterflies of anxiety attack, stop and analyze their source. Are they based on fact or vague premonitions? Is the fear "real" or just your "what if" worries? On a blank piece of paper, mark off three columns: My Fears; Facts They Are Based On; and, What I Can Do. When you identify a fact-based fear write how you can respond or who you will need to help you. Draw a line through the free-floating fears and promise to give them to the Lord.

Prayer

O God, I trust in you. My Jesus, I believe in your word. Holy Spirit, I rest in the comfort and protection of your presence. Holy Trinity, be with me to scatter the fears of my soul and to strengthen me in the grace of your everlasting care. Amen.

Scripture for Reflection

The Lord is my shepherd, there is nothing I shall lack.

Psalms 23:1

Journaling

What thoughts, feelings and prayers are in your heart right now?

—11—

Overwhelmed by Details

*T*here is no way to prepare for the number of details that attack the average widow struggling to hold body, mind and soul together. They can be staggering, bewildering and frightening.

Tell the children, notify relatives and friends, contact the funeral home and church, gather clothing, fill out forms with their hundreds of details, select a casket, order flowers, arrange for out-of-towners, buy extra groceries, clean the house, deal with musicians, contact insurance companies, the VA, government and other work-related groups, prepare and submit an obituary. And this is for just the first few days following death.

Notice, that this list does not include grieve, struggle to get up each day, force yourself to eat, weep, rage against fate, try to sleep, pray. These details, because they aren't on a neat checklist, may get shoved to the bottom of your to-do list, or not happen at all. We think the activities on this list will happen automatically because they seem beyond our control, instinctual activities. Pay attention, for they are the most important tasks of grief work to which you must attend.

Don't let the busyness of decision-making and the weariness of emotional fatigue hold you back from doing the most important work of your life . . . grieving.

Action

In the midst of the myriad details of life following the death of a spouse . . . allow time in your day for grief to express itself in whatever way it comes.

Prayer

Lord of simplicity, you who created order out of chaos and brought harmony to the universe, pour your grace on me in the midst of this turmoil and stress. Help me to clear my mind while I deal with the many details of death. Keep my heart calm though all around me seems out of control. Give me wisdom to recognize that the details of life can be handled one item at a time, one day at a time . . . and the most important detail is to mourn my husband. Amen.

Scripture for Reflection

The Lord answered her: "Martha, Martha, you are anxious and upset about many things, when only one thing is necessary. Mary has chosen the better part, and it will not be taken away from her."   Luke 10:41-42

Journaling

What thoughts, feelings and prayers are in your heart right now?

Loneliness

*U*nderstanding Adam's feelings of loneliness as the only human creature led God to create Eve.

Loneliness is the universal emotion of unchosen aloneness. It is being alone when you want to be with others. It is forced aloneness, the feeling that painfully wrings your heart with the thought that you are alone in the world and this will never change.

Where once you had a partner and companion, now you are alone. Where there was someone for whom you were the center of the universe, now there is no one in whose intimacy you find fulfillment. Where once you could lean securely on another human being, having tested them and found them trustworthy, now it seems you face the uncertainties of life on your own, wondering in whom to place your trust.

Everyone experiences loneliness, which can be debilitating unless you learn to convert it into solitude, an ability to relish your own company and use your aloneness to indulge yourself in prayer and self-regard, in comfort, friendship and well-being.

Eventually, loneliness will dissipate and the fruits of solitude will compel you to reach out to others.

Action

If you are lonely just now, reflect on how you might change that to solitude. Do you enjoy music, reading, artistic work? Indulge yourself. Do you have a place that uplifts your spirit, like a garden or park? Go there and spend time with nature, grateful for God's creation. Find within your own spirit and your deepening relationship with God the avenue to connection with the world around you and with your own inner reservoir of strength.

Prayer

Sweet Jesus, you too experienced loneliness. You wept in the garden because you saw the cross in your future. You found in solitary prayer, the companionship of God, who would not let you walk your journey alone. Turn your eyes to me now. I fear being swallowed up in my loneliness. Grant me the grace to recognize my inner strength. Walk with me, as the Father walked with you, and reveal to me how my loneliness can become the gift of blessed solitude. In your name, I pray. Amen.

Scripture for Reflection

"Father, if you are willing, take this cup from me. Yet not my will but yours be done." Then an angel from heaven appeared to him and gave him strength.   Luke 22:42-43

Journaling

What thoughts, feelings and prayers are in your heart right now?

An Empty Hand, An Aching Body

Sexual love and the desire to be touched and held lovingly don't die with a spouse. It is normal and natural to yearn for the physical love of your husband, and to wonder if anyone will ever hold you close again.

Sexual love isn't the only body-contact widows miss. Every couple shares intimate physical signs of love not replicated with others: holding hands as you take a walk; an arm around the shoulders as you sit and talk; a quick kiss before parting for a day's activities. The hole left when these loving gestures are gone seems unfillable.

Some widows are tempted to seek sexual gratification randomly because while unready for or uninterested in another commitment, they have a deep need for physical contact and signs of loving union. Since we are whole persons, and our bodies, minds and spirits are one—not neat, separate compartments—to engage in sexual love without commitment and care, is not only dangerous to your health; but also, to your spiritual nature and integrity.

Acknowledging the need for physical contact and loving touch is an important step. Asking family and friends for hugs and appropriate gestures of affection is the next. You can do it.

Action

Express your concerns, needs and struggles first to your-self. If you journal, write about your feelings. Talk with trusted family members or friends about your need for affection and physical signs of love. Take the first step by reaching out appropriately to others. Nothing will replace the love of your husband, but that doesn't mean you must live without affection in the days to come.

Prayer

Jesus, I yearn for the loving touch and attention of my husband. I miss his warm embrace, our companionable walks hand-in-hand, the love of our sexual union. Quiet my anxieties, comfort me with your presence and help me to reach out with affection to others.

Be with me, Jesus, as I learn to live my life as a responsi-ble single woman. Amen.

Scripture for Reflection

When Jesus saw her, he called her forward and said, "Woman, you are freed from your infirmity." Then he laid his hands on her, and immediately she stood up straight and began praising God.   Luke 13:12-13

Journaling

What thoughts, feelings and prayers are in your heart right now?

What to Do with Guilt

*D*id I listen well enough to his concerns? Could I have done more? Why wasn't I more patient and understanding? Many widows review the final days, weeks, months or years of their marriage with a mixture of gratitude, love and guilt.

Guilt, a common emotion, can be rational or irrational. When you knowingly hurt or harm another, guilt is rational, based on something factual and controllable. When you feel guilty about experiences over which you had no control or, were unable to find alternative responses, the guilt may be irrational. In either form, but especially with irrational guilt experienced after a death, you are robbed of inner peace and the ability to mourn your husband without recrimination and "what ifs."

If times were difficult, or you were a stressed caregiver; if he died suddenly and there were words or deeds left undone or unresolved, you may feel guilty because you didn't measure up to your own standards. But remember, you did the best you could with what you knew and with the resources available to you at the time.

Rational guilt has its place, especially when it leads to remorse and determination to do better the next time. Irrational guilt should be tossed out, quickly.

Action

If you experience guilt, write a letter to your husband expressing your feelings and describing the situations at the root of your guilt. Express your remorse and ask for his forgiveness. Offer your forgiveness, as well, for anything he may have left undone or unsaid that could have given you an easier mind and heart. Place the letter in a special place for a few days. When you return to it, burn it in a metal bowl and bury the ashes outside, along with the guilt. It's time to move on.

Prayer

Gentle and loving God, help me to forgive myself for all the mistakes I made in my marriage, for the times I wasn't all I could be and the harsh or unkind words I can never take back. Show me that my loved one forgave me long ago for not being perfect. He loved me as I am. May this knowledge, and your grace, release the guilt that lies on my heart and place there instead a sure understanding of your love and forgiveness. Amen.

Scripture for Reflection

The Lord redeems the lives of those who serve him; no one will be condemned who takes refuge in him.

Psalms 34:23

Journaling

What thoughts, feelings and prayers are in your heart right now?

Clinging to Prayer as a Support and Refuge

*E*verything changed when your husband died. It may feel like a tidal wave has overtaken you, or an earthquake knocked you off your feet and sent you sprawling. Is there nothing to which you can cling? Is there no one whose enduring support you can count on?

These thoughts and feelings were also expressed by the psalmist and Job. Take comfort in their writings because in their laments you see souls unafraid to throw themselves on the Lord, with faith in his response.

Prayer, the lifting of your mind and heart to God, is truly the glue that binds you to this world and gives you entry into the next. Prayer comes in many forms; the simple, spontaneous words of conversation with God, formal prayers in a book, corporate prayer with a community, the unspoken, silent prayer of the heart. The form is unimportant; prayer is the rock on which you can build your life.

In prayer you meet the One whose presence is healing and whose love is unconditional. In prayer you find the One who knows your needs, is comfortable with your tears and does not hide from your distress. God is the one who yearns to give you all that your heart desires.

Action

If you do not already have a time of prayer set aside in your day, begin today. At first you may only have a time of quiet. Later, you might use a prayer book or read the scriptures as a starting point. Eventually, as you are faithful to your time with God, you will find your heart expressing its deepest thoughts and feelings and receiving the response of One who knows you inside-out.

Prayer

Father, Son and Holy Spirit, give me the words to tell you what it feels like to be a widow, how much I miss my husband. Help me to spill the thoughts and feelings of my heart and to leave time and room to listen to your response. Offer me a glimpse of your strength and unconditional regard. Let me cling to you in my mourning so that I might rejoice with you in the days to come. Amen.

Scripture for Reflection

You have made the Lord your refuge and chosen the Most High to be your dwelling. Therefore, no evil will threaten you, no calamity will come near your dwelling.

Psalms 91:9-10

Journaling

What thoughts, feelings and prayers are in your heart right now?

Forgiveness

*W*idows reflect often on the past. Instead of endlessly dusting memories, let your reflection bear fruit. One of the fruits some widows hesitate to embrace is consciously choosing to forgive their husbands whatever faults or offenses they may have committed, especially those that damaged family life and/or marriage.

While forgiveness is hard for us, God forgives everything. You see this in the way Jesus offered mercy and love to all, especially sinners. If all of heaven rejoices over the repentance of one sinner—what kind of celebration must occur when someone chooses to forgive, a quality so God-like in nature?

To forgive is to go beyond your self—to give more than is expected. Forgiveness will have a greater effect on your life than on the one forgiven. It frees your soul from unnecessary burdens and expands your spirit to walk more closely with God. It isn't a matter of "what was done," or "who is right," but a generous gift of compassion mirroring the mercy God has already shown to you.

You cannot expect from God what you are not willing to give to others. Give forgiveness. You won't regret it.

Action

Write your husband a letter offering him your forgiveness. Be specific about what it is you are forgiving. Bring the letter to your prayer and offer it to God, a love-offering to both your husband and the Lord; a loving gesture of kindness toward yourself.

Prayer

Lord, why is it so difficult to let go of hurt and offer forgiveness? Why do I want to cling to the hurts of the past rather than free myself to look forward to the future? Blessed One, sting my heart with the power of your love, reveal to me your Sacred Heart, wounded yet filled with love. Give me the grace to forgive and the peace that is its reward. Amen.

Scripture for Reflection

Do not judge, and you will not be judged. Do not condemn, and you will not be condemned. Forgive, and you will be forgiven.   Luke 6:37

Journaling

What thoughts, feelings and prayers are in your heart right now?

I'm Angry and I Don't Want to Be

*W*hy is it that anger overtakes you when you are least able to defend yourself against it? Your husband is dead and the life you planned together is no longer an option. The sacrifices made, the obstacles overcome, the love shared is all a piece of your past now; the future you envisioned together is with him in the grave. That alone is enough to make you angry, to wonder about fairness, to question God's judgment.

But anger is a strange emotion; it isn't always blatant. Sometimes it's subtle and looks like exhaustion, irritability, sarcasm, or depression. Anger is just an emotion, but it has a powerful kick and ignoring it can produce unwanted emotional, social and physical consequences.

Most people don't choose to be angry. They want to have good relationships with others and to feel at ease in the world. If you recognize anger in your speech, actions or thoughts, act fast to understand its source and choose to dismantle it. You do have choices about your response to life and daily events, don't let anger eat away at positive possibilities. Instead, remember the merciful and gracious kindness of God and resolve to offer that kind of love to yourself and others.

Action

Anger is a good emotion to journal about. When you experience anger, even provoked by something real, you have at least two choices: let it go and respond in a way that affirms your values, or name your anger and talk it out. The old advice of "counting to ten" before responding is actually very healthy. Deep breaths help too. Never go to bed angry; instead, release your anger to God, in prayer, and ask for guidance in shaping your response.

Prayer

Jesus, you knew all the human emotions, including anger. Feeling angry can be justified, but an angry response that is destructive of others, is not. I don't want to approach life as an angry person. Give me the grace to understand my emotions, to heal my self-esteem and to choose life-giving responses that affirm my values and faith. Amen.

Scripture for Reflection

The Lord is merciful and gracious, slow to anger and abounding in kindness.   Psalms 103:8

Journaling

What thoughts, feelings and prayers are in your heart right now?

Being Single in a Couple's World

*O*nce you were two, now you are one . . . again. No matter the time since you were a single woman, one thing
is for sure, in a world full of committed couples, or people
looking to be coupled or bemoaning their singleness, being
single in a coupled world takes some getting used to.

Simple things like going to a show, having someone to
zip the back of your dress, an extra pair of hands to hold the
ladder, a dancing partner whose moves you know, a dinner
companion after a long day, suddenly become logistics'
exercises.

The taken-for-granted presence of another becomes a
vast emptiness each time you see a couple riding in a car,
shopping, dining, or at church. Each reminder redefines the
loss of your own missing partner. On every occasion you are
not invited to join your coupled friends, your singleness
becomes an anchor, weighing you down.

Rather than doom, this new singleness signals the need
for adjustment. It may take cultivating new interests and
new friends, but eventually, as you learn to re-navigate the
world around you, solo, you will regain your confidence.
While you may always miss the sweet togetherness of being
part of a married couple, you may be surprised at how your
singleness opens new doors and new adventures.

Action

Rather than lament your single status, take some initiative. Make a list of the things you've always wanted to do but haven't done. Maybe it's a trip, a class, a special talent you never pursued, an education put on hold . . . whatever the dream, now might be the time to indulge it. Need new friends? Join a group that corresponds to your interests, volunteer, sing in the choir. You'll only lament being single if you see it as a curse rather than as a blessing.

Prayer

O God, I loved being part of a couple. I was comfortable and I'm not ready to be single again. Open my eyes to see this new time in my life as a blessing in disguise. Help me to unwrap the package of my singleness and discover there the rich opportunities you have in store for me. Give me courage to move forward alone and wisdom to make choices that will lead me into genuine relationships with others and with you. Amen.

Scripture for Reflection

Take delight in the Lord, and he will grant you what your heart desires.   Psalms 37:4

Journaling

What thoughts, feelings and prayers are in your heart right now?

A Daily Dose of Strength and Courage

*T*he alarm rings. You open your eyes to light bombarding your windows. The urge to stay in bed, turn over and avoid this new day is smothered by the sun, eager to offer you a dose of strength and courage. You arise.

Most of our waking is not this idyllic. Most often, you wake, rub your eyes, confirm that it isn't too early and lumber your way into the new day. But if you stop to think, the gift of a new day brings with it a promise of what is needed to make that day worth living.

It is said that God does not give you more than you can handle. While you may carp at that thought, giving examples to disprove it, the fact is that you can only live one day at a time, morning 'til night, whether or not you think you can.

The miracle of this rhythm is a witness to grace, and grace is always a dose of strength and courage. So when you are tempted to complain that you are too weak to continue the journey, or too unhappy to see beauty and goodness around you, remember your daily dose of strength and courage and leap forward to catch the sun.

Action

When you awake today, whether it is sunny or grey, give praise to God for yet another new day of strength and courage and offer yourself as a testimony to the miracle of grace.

Prayer

I praise you God of sunlight and evening moon. I reach out my heart to you, opening it to receive all the strength and courage you send my way this day. I thank you for your steadfast love and the grace of a new day to find my way. Amen.

Scripture for Reflection

Shout joyfully to God, all the earth; sing the glory of his name; offer to him glorious praise. Say to God: "How awesome are your deeds!"   Psalms 66:1-3

Journaling

What thoughts, feelings and prayers are in your heart right now?

What Should I Do with His Things?

*I*n the end, your husband's life is reduced to two things: those who love and remember him and his "things."

If there are children, they will want a memento—an article of clothing, piece of jewelry, a rosary or prayer book, recording, picture or collector's piece. It's wise to allow your children or grandchildren to choose the items of remembrance they wish to have . . . first taking out those with which you are not ready to part.

Afterward, deciding what to keep and how to dispose of the rest will loom large. Some widows rid themselves of everything very quickly and regret their haste. Others keep their husband's closet just as it was for many months or even years, unable to part with these last physical remnants of his life. Some share good items with thrift stores or those in need. Some make quilts, pillows and stuffed animals from his clothing. The options are as many as there are widows and none is wrong or right.

Whatever your situation, keep this in mind: you carry your husband in your heart and in your memory. You are tied to him by the mysterious and unbreakable bonds of marriage. Whatever you decide to do with his things will never remove his presence within you.

Action

Sort your husband's things taking out those you want to keep for awhile—watches/rings, clothing to make a quilt or pillow, special items of remembrance. Put these in a storage container. Invite your family to choose those things they would like to keep. Then let yourself rest. When you are ready, decide how you will dispose of what remains. There is no hurry.

Prayer

Dear Lord, I dread having to parcel out my dear one's things, yet the pain of seeing them pierces my heart. Please be my companion as I sort through his belongings. Sit by my side as I lovingly touch each item. Wipe away the tears that will surely fall. Bless my heart with joy of remembrance and my face with a smile of tenderness as I do this last act for him.

Grant me wisdom to dispose of his things in a way that honors his life. Amen.

Scripture for Reflection

Looking at him, Jesus was moved with love and said, "You need to do one further thing. Go and sell what you own, and give to the poor, and you will have treasure in heaven. Then come, follow me."   Mark 10:21

Journaling

What thoughts, feelings and prayers are in your heart right now?

Joy Breaks Through

*J*oy is different from happiness. It is a deeper, less fleeting quality; a gift of the Holy Spirit. It isn't something manufactured or an activity, person or prayer you conjure up. Joy is inner contentment and purpose, in spite of distressing or sad circumstances. It comes from belief in God's faithful presence and provision for your future.

While joy seems elusive or vague, it is ever-present within you and attainable. It superimposes itself over distress; sorrow cannot crush it and grief cannot triumph over it. Jesus certainly knew disappointment, sorrow, grief and confusion, yet he also knew that his father loved him, was ever-present to him and would not allow him to perish without a future. Jesus understood joy, that deeper peace that overcame his outward situation and was fed by faith.

So, the question remains, what is joy? Joy is the foundation for hope and spurs you to increased love of God and others. Your joy affects the lives of those who recognize your contentment in any and all circumstances and want this same joy in their lives.

Action

Keep track of two things: the moments when joy breaks in and you experience calm or peace even in trying circumstances; and, the "joy-breakers," those people, situations and thoughts that rob you of your inner calm and belief in God's loving presence and purpose for your life. Obviously, cling to the moments of joy and eliminate the joy-breakers.

Prayer

Jesus, your life was not without sorrow, pain, and grief. Yet, you lived with a calm trust in God that attracted others to you. Teach me to recognize the gift of joy that the Spirit has given me. Teach me to claim my joy and have gratitude for it. Increase my faith and hope and let my joy break through so that others may be led to you and each circumstance of life can become a window into your love and peace. Amen.

Scripture for Reflection

They were filled with fear and great joy, and they ran from the tomb to inform his disciples.

Matthew 28:8

Journaling

What thoughts, feelings and prayers are in your heart right now?

Holidays and Special Occasions

*H*olidays produce enough stress without the added aspect of widowhood. You may feel like the only person in the world who doesn't want to celebrate. You might force yourself "for the sake of others," but endure with a heavy heart. You may even dread festive events. You aren't the first or only one to feel like this. You will survive.

Why do holidays, anniversaries, birthdays, weddings, new babies and such impact us so powerfully during our mourning period? Simply, because each occasion highlights that as family and friends gather, there is an empty place at the table, someone whose life and joy is missing. Each occasion emphasizes that you have suffered an irreversible loss that no gift or happy gathering can bring back.

The annual cycle of events needs to run its course. It is part of the healing process. Do what you can, in your own way. Feel free to postpone entertaining or travel. Listen to your own needs and ask others to respect them as well. Each successive year's events will be more tolerable, more anticipated, less distressing. It is the nature of things, this cycle. Your heart will learn to absorb its wound and open a new space for joy and merriment.

Action

Make a plan as each holiday or special occasion approaches. Where will you be, with whom will you spend the day, how do you want to acknowledge the occasion? Making a plan takes some of the dread off the occasion and gives you a measure of control, which in turn helps to stabilize your emotional response. Don't wait until the day comes, do it now.

Prayer

Lord, is there any way to live this year without the holidays? Can I have a new calendar that eliminates all events it seems too hard to bear alone? I feel like such a weakling . . . dreading what used to be happy and exciting times. Give me the courage to honor my feelings and to choose how I want to experience holidays and special occasions this year. Stand by me as I allow both my joy and my distress to become sources of self-knowledge and strength. Amen.

Scripture for Reflection

Amen, amen, I say to you, you will weep and mourn, while the world rejoices. You will be sorrowful, but your grief will turn into joy.   John 16:20

Journaling

What thoughts, feelings and prayers are in your heart right now?

I Can't Do This by Myself . . . Can I?

*W*idowhood is harsh in its day after day relentlessness. If only you could mourn for a week or month and be finished. If only you didn't wake and sleep with a heavy heart, fearing when you will dissolve in tears or be gripped by "the blues." If you are a young widow, sheltering and supporting your children compounds the difficulty. Being a widow isn't for the faint of heart.

Many widows are overwhelmed by the emotional work involved in widowhood. They look for help from support groups, church, family and friends. They think others will make the grief easier to bear, even as they bemoan their own inability to "spring back, quickly." While groups and outside help are important aids in the grief process, nothing can do your grief work for you. Only you can live each day with all its emotions and challenges, until you have healed.

Though a husband's death can batter your self-esteem, the truth is you can care for yourself. You do know what is best for your life and what helps you to deal positively with your grief. Coping with this life-transition can be frightening, but you have handled other challenges in the past and you can triumph over this challenge, too.

Action

Keep a daily journal of your feelings, thoughts, fears and successes. List the people you find helpful, the feelings that are problematic, issues that challenge your skills and who you might ask for help. Then one by one, ask for the help you need; and celebrate the things you can do for yourself.

Prayer

God of all creation, show me the way. Facing the future alone is daunting, Lord, and I'm not sure I can do it; but with you at my side, walking each step of the way with me, I believe I can create a new life. Bless me with your presence, Lord, and grant me the confidence to become the person you want me to be. Amen.

Scripture for Reflection

I can do all things in him who strengthens me.

Philippians 4:13

Journaling

What thoughts, feelings and prayers are in your heart right now?

24

Feeling Desperate and Depressed

*F*eeling sad, "tied up in knots," empty of purpose? Fighting insomnia? Are you crushingly tired or unusually withdrawn, unwilling to engage with others? Are you despondent, rundown, dispirited, or weak? It may be that you are depressed.

In simple terms, depression is anger turned inward and often occurs when you aren't able to control your environment. It can take a mild form, like feeling "down in the dumps;" or, be more severe causing you to isolate yourself from others. In any form, it causes you to look at your world from a negative viewpoint, where there is nothing good in the world, including yourself.

At the first signs of depression, seek out a doctor to check for any physical problems. If you are physically healthy, look for a support group and/or counselor. Talking about what bothers you and sharing your experience and feelings with others can take the edge off depression, letting the inner gloom out into the light where it can heal and set you on a more positive course.

If depression sets in, don't panic; it happens to everyone at some time and for lesser reasons. Understanding the nature of depression and how to deal with it offers perspective and the steps necessary to overcome it.

Action

Your perception of depression will help you keep it at bay. Recognize it as just another emotion, not something that will overpower you. If you notice signs of depression, don't be embarrassed or afraid. Seek out help and take medication as prescribed by your doctor.

Prayer

Jesus, when you wept in the garden, were you experiencing depression? Did you feel the same desolation and emptiness I feel? You went to prayer, and pouring out your heart to your Father, you found comfort and peace. Guide me in recognizing my depression for what it is . . . an inner cry for help. Help me to pray in confidence for the strength to meet life's challenges, to surround myself with others who will support me, and to seek help when I need it. Be my light whenever darkness threatens to overcome me. Amen.

Scripture for Reflection

For surely I know the plans I have for you, says the Lord, plans for your welfare and not for harm, to give you a future with hope. Then when you call upon me and come and pray to me, I will hear you. When you search for me, you will find me; if you seek me with all your heart.

Jeremiah 29: 11-13

Journaling

What thoughts, feelings and prayers are in your heart right now?

25

This Isn't Normal–Or Is It?

*I*s it normal to want to live and die at the same time?

Unfortunately, when you are a widow, this and so much more, is normal.

Widows often experience an incoherent rush of thoughts and feelings that don't seem to be in sync with anything—except, mourning. They wonder if what they are thinking or feeling, as bizarre as it sometimes seems, has ever been experienced by others. The answer is bittersweet: yes and no.

The good news is that widows share this kaleidoscope of feelings because the complexity and intensity are particular to grief. No one is alone in this. On the other hand, each widow faces her period of grief uniquely. All the books in the world won't describe exactly what each widow endures. So the down side is that each must learn to navigate the waters of grief on her own. That doesn't mean that others can't be helpful or point you in a good direction or empathize with your experience. But what is normal can only be decided by you.

Having said that, beware of self-destructive thoughts or actions, decisions that involve hurting others, or relationships that become dependent or abusive. These aren't normal, whether you're grieving or not.

Action

Flip through magazines you may subscribe to, or your newspaper. Over the course of several days or months, cut out pictures or words that describe what you are experiencing. When you are ready, buy a poster board, piece of foam core or even a canvas, and paste or decoupage your words and pictures into a harmonious collage of what is "normal" for you during your mourning.

Prayer

Holy Angels of God, be with me as I sort out my thoughts and feelings. Sprinkle me with angel dust and inspire me to understand that everything I thought was normal is no longer . . . yet what I am thinking and feeling now, is my new normal. Grant me your exquisite "lightness of being," to give myself room to change, to grow, to just "be" in this new world without the man I love. Amen.

Scripture for Reflection

The Lord will fulfill his plan for me. Your kindness, O Lord, endures forever; do not forsake the work of your hands.   Psalms 138:8

Journaling

What thoughts, feelings and prayers are in your heart right now?

26

I Felt His Presence Today

$\mathcal{S}$ome widows think they see their husbands, or hear him in the shower, turning a key in the lock, or walking on the stairs. Others hear him calling their names, or see him shopping at the mall. These can be disturbing experiences if you aren't prepared for them. You may wonder if you are losing your mind.

Other widows say they "felt his presence," particularly during an especially trying time or on a special occasion or when in need. The literature on grieving abounds with such stories, assuring us that they are normal experiences for some people. This external demonstration of your internal mourning passes with time.

We believe in the communion of saints, that we are united with those who have gone before us. Their spirits are never far from us, as available to us after death as their physical presence was available in life. Don't be afraid to talk with your husband, to share your daily experiences or ask him to help you through your grief.

As you feel your husband's presence, in faith, acknowledge the presence of God, who upholds your life and in whose glorious presence your husband now resides.

Action

If you have a visual or auditory experience of your husband, don't panic. Stop for a minute and say a prayer that his spirit is at rest. Offer your gratitude for this moment of remembrance.

Prayer

Sweet Mother Mary, did you see Joseph after he died? Could you still hear his voice calling from his carpenter shop? Free me to fill my heart with good thoughts and to pray for my husband's peace. Comfort me as a mother comforts her daughter, a friend embraces her friend. You were a widow, too, show me the way. Amen.

Scripture for Reflection

The Lord, your God, is in your midst, a warrior who gives victory; he will rejoice over you with gladness, he will renew you in his love; he will exult over you with loud singing.   Zephaniah 3:17

Journaling

What thoughts, feelings and prayers are in your heart right now?

27

God, I Am Grateful

*W*idows recognize with gratitude each image of love, support and happiness that flashes across the screens of their minds. Without these moments of joy, fun, and loving kindness, life would have been so much less fulfilling.

What takes more time, is expressing gratitude for the hard times, for the unkind words spoken in anger, the unkept promises, the sorrows and unfulfilled dreams. While harder to be grateful for worries or distress, character flaws that brought heartache and loss, it's still important to give thanks.

The demanding periods in your marriage developed your inner strength and taught you that you could survive, could forgive and rise above yourself for the sake of others. It was the challenges that tested your resolve, commitment and faith and threw you to your knees to rely on God's wisdom and grace. Each time, God's power worked in you and raised you up.

Giving thanks to God should be part of every day, easy or hard; joyous or sad. Today is no harder than yesterday or tomorrow, and the grace of God that sustained you in the past will uphold you today and bless you tomorrow. That is reason enough to lift a grateful heart.

Action

Make a gratitude box that you keep in your prayer space or anywhere you can easily see and access it. In the box, each day, place a piece of paper on which you write things for which you are grateful. You can do it as many times as you like throughout the day. Each week, go through your box and read your gratitude list. Have you been grateful for the challenging times as well?

Prayer

God of every day, I give you thanks and praise for each and every joy and sorrow I encounter today. I praise you for the hard times in my past for I now recognize your abundant blessings, sustaining me and giving me life. I thank you for my present, difficult as it is, for I realize you are guiding me into a new life. I adore you for the future you are building for me, a life full of the richness of your presence. Amen.

Scripture for Reflection

Give thanks in all circumstances; for this is the will of God for you in Christ Jesus.   1 Thessalonians 5:18

Journaling

What thoughts, feelings and prayers are in your heart right now?

28

Laughter

A sense of humor is a gift planted deep within each person, a magic tonic; it keeps you healthy and balanced during even the most difficult times.

Research indicates that laughter has both preventative and therapeutic values. Laughter enriches the blood with oxygen and increases deep breathing, as well as removes the negative effects of stress and helps to boost the immune system. It helps to control high blood pressure, increases stamina, alleviates pain, squelches depression and anxiety and aids in sleep. And, it's free. With all these benefits, why don't we laugh more?

It may not seem there is much to laugh about at present, yet the idiosyncrasies and ironies of life go unchanged, just waiting to be noticed. Once you look at life through the lens of humor, you'll never want to go back. You'll sensitize your "funny bone" and begin to see that not everything in life is a cause for tragedy and concern; some things are just plain funny and no matter your situation in life, your mental and spiritual health need to acknowledge that.

It has been shown that laughter helps the heart. That alone should motivate widows to seek out times of laughter, for the brokenhearted need healing like no others.

Action

Try to build up your "laughter factor." Watch funny movies and TV programs; read books by well-known comedians. Go out of your way to have a good laugh . . . even if it means listening to corny jokes. Observe the absurd and incongruous around you. Watch infants and children and animals. Make friends with funny people. Remind yourself to have fun. Avoid people, conversations and news that frighten, upset or distress you.

Prayer

Jesus, you must have laughed at the foibles of your disciples and at the children who clamored to sit with you. Did you laugh with your parents as you learned new things? Laughter doesn't come to me as easily these days, yet I'm tired of tears. Give me back the gift of laughter. Help me to look at life with an eye to the ridiculous. Heal me of my gloom and brighten my face with a smile . . . if only, at my own inability to laugh. Amen.

Scripture for Reflection

We are fools for the sake of Christ . . .

1 Corinthians 4:10

Journaling

What thoughts, feelings and prayers are in your heart right now?

29

Reaching Out to Life

*I*t may be weeks, months or years since your husband died. You've done your fair share of crying, struggling to regain your equilibrium, and handling life affairs by yourself. You've changed some things and held on to others. You have survived. Now, you feel a surge of inner life that tells you it's time to reach out with renewed energy and clearer focus, to take a more active stance in shaping your future.

Mourning periods are different for each person, so there are no guarantees that you will be ready to revamp your life and engage in it more fully at any pre-determined time. It is a "wait and see," "test the waters a bit at a time" kind of venture; an experience of listening deeply to your inner self and to the wisdom God plants there. You may have tried some small steps, like going out with friends, or joining a club or class; but avoided the big steps, like deciding to downsize, or to move to another city or state, or to begin dating.

Eventually, your internal clock (not some outside source) will tell you that it's time for the bigger decisions. Listen to it. Life is a gift to be unwrapped and celebrated daily.

Action

Make a list of the "big" decisions and dreams you find in your heart. Circle the ones that need some professional advice and jot the name of someone you might ask. Of the others, which one jumps out at you and says, "Deal with me, first!" Do it.

Prayer

Holy Spirit, giver of life, thank you for this surge of life within me. Something new wants to be born and I have only to nurture and protect it in order to bring it to birth. Guide my days of pondering and prayer. Fill me with wisdom and an abiding trust in you. Let my joy be as deep and penetrating as my sorrow has been and as it springs forth, may I radiate your life within me to all I meet. Amen.

Scripture for Reflection

Therefore my heart is glad and my soul rejoices; my body too is filled with confidence . . . You will show me the path to life; you will fill me with joy in your presence.

Psalms 16:9, 11

Journaling

What thoughts, feelings and prayers are in your heart right now?

30

Rainbows After the Flood

*O*ne of the most poignant and beautiful scriptural images is of God placing a rainbow in the sky as a reminder of his faithful covenant with humanity. Noah trusted God enough to build an ark with no storm in sight, to gather the remnants of his life and family and take a journey without a clear destination. Noah trusted in spite of storms, difficult people and situations, and overwhelming fear. He trusted and finally God brought him to a safe place where he could rebuild his life.

To reward Noah's trust, God painted a rainbow as a promise of his ongoing care. Its beauty continues to remind us that God's presence never leaves those he loves, and even the darkest days are only a flimsy cover for beauty hidden just beneath. The rainbow invites you to believe in the God who never fails; in the wonderful things God has in store for those who love God.

You've battled your own flood these days and months and hopefully experienced some rainbows, too. No matter what the future brings, one glance at a rainbow is a powerful reminder that God is walking this journey with you, faithful at every moment, and especially during the storms.

Action

Whenever it rains, think about the rainbow. Walk outside and look to where the rain mingles with the sun, painting its bow in the sky. Say a quick prayer of trust in God's faithfulness and in appreciation for this sign of his presence.

Prayer

O God, you are the faithful one. When I am tempted to doubt, you give me a sign of your love. It might be a friend's call, or a note in the mail, a song or even, a rainbow. Your goodness overpowers me and my heart is filled with gratitude and love. Amen.

Scripture for Reflection

I have set my bow in the clouds, and it shall be a sign of the covenant between me and the earth.   Genesis 9:13

Journaling

What thoughts, feelings and prayers are in your heart right now?